British Library Cataloguing in Publication Data

The Twelve days of Christmas. — (Square books)
   1. Carols, English — Text
   I. Langton, Roger
   783.6´52   PR1195.C2
   ISBN 0-7214-9580-X

First edition

Published by Ladybird Books Ltd Loughborough Leicestershire UK
Ladybird Books Inc Lewiston Maine 04240 USA

Printed in England

The twelve days of Christmas

illustrated by Roger Langton

Ladybird Books

On the first day of Christmas
my true love sent to me,
a partridge in a pear tree.

On the second day of Christmas
my true love sent to me,
two turtledoves
and a partridge in a pear tree.

On the third day of Christmas
my true love sent to me,
three French hens,
two turtledoves
and a partridge in a pear tree.

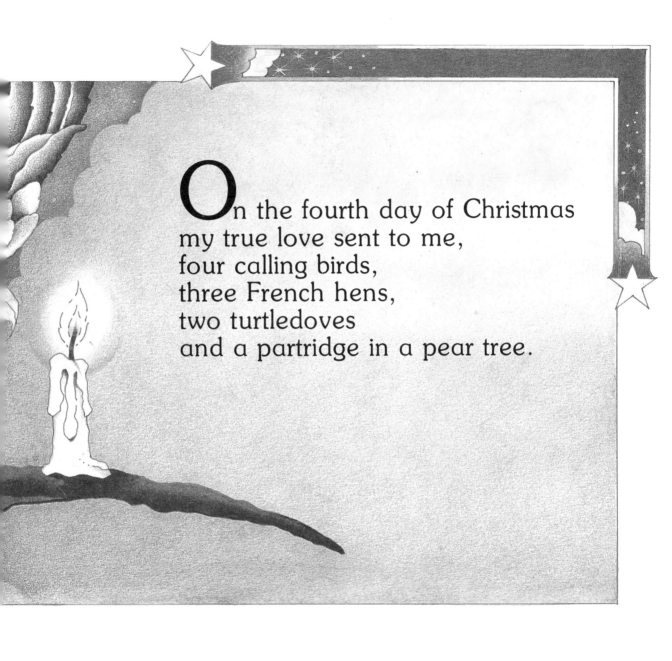

On the fourth day of Christmas
my true love sent to me,
four calling birds,
three French hens,
two turtledoves
and a partridge in a pear tree.

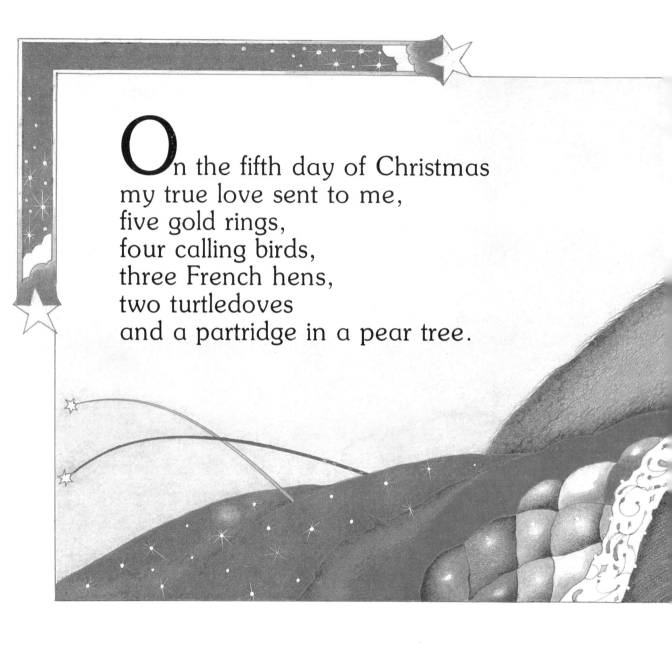

On the fifth day of Christmas
my true love sent to me,
five gold rings,
four calling birds,
three French hens,
two turtledoves
and a partridge in a pear tree.

On the sixth day of Christmas
my true love sent to me,
six geese a-laying,
five gold rings,
four calling birds,
three French hens,
two turtledoves
and a partridge in a pear tree.

On the seventh day of Christmas
my true love sent to me,
seven swans a-swimming,
six geese a-laying,
five gold rings,
four calling birds,
three French hens,
two turtledoves
and a partridge in a pear tree.

On the eighth day of Christmas
my true love sent to me,
eight maids a-milking,
seven swans a-swimming,
six geese a-laying,
five gold rings,
four calling birds,
three French hens,
two turtledoves
and a partridge in a pear tree.

On the ninth day of Christmas
my true love sent to me,
nine ladies dancing,
eight maids a-milking,
seven swans a-swimming,
six geese a-laying,
five gold rings,
four calling birds,
three French hens,
two turtledoves
and a partridge in a pear tree.

On the tenth day of Christmas
my true love sent to me,
ten lords a-leaping,
nine ladies dancing,
eight maids a-milking,
seven swans a-swimming,
six geese a-laying,
five gold rings,
four calling birds,
three French hens,
two turtledoves
and a partridge in a pear tree.

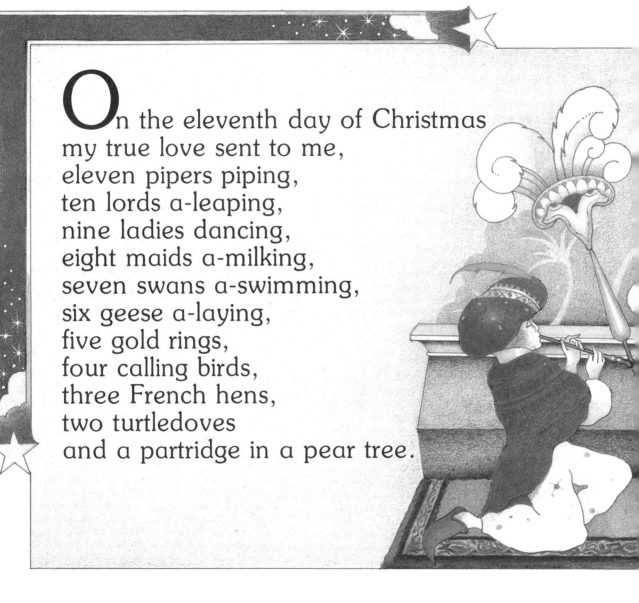

On the eleventh day of Christmas
my true love sent to me,
eleven pipers piping,
ten lords a-leaping,
nine ladies dancing,
eight maids a-milking,
seven swans a-swimming,
six geese a-laying,
five gold rings,
four calling birds,
three French hens,
two turtledoves
and a partridge in a pear tree.

On the twelfth day of Christmas
my true love sent to me,
twelve drummers drumming,
eleven pipers piping,
ten lords a-leaping,
nine ladies dancing,
eight maids a-milking,
seven swans a-swimming,
six geese a-laying,
five gold rings,
four calling birds,
three French hens,
two turtledoves
and a partridge in a pear tree.